People Watching

Amber Furuya

Presentation by *BookLeaf Publishing*

Web: www.bookleafpub.com

E-mail: info@bookleafpub.com

ISBN: 978-93-95755-32-0

First edition 2022

for the people watchers

An introduction

This is the story
Written in disguise
Of hidden pain and memories
As seen by my eyes

This is the story
Of blood sweat and fears
Collected together
Over the last 19 years

Train Tracks

I can see you're nervousness
As the train breaks
The way you beat your own heart against your
chest
As if in that second, if your heart stopped
From the crash of metal
Fear against your face
That it would beat again

But both you and I know if it were to come to
that
The chaos of sirens and bells
The final stop
We would be pleasured with silence
Fulfilling our deepest desires

Alignment

He stood watching the stars
Remembering the last moment
When the planets aligned
A moment in which pain became grief
And when grief became contentment

But it was different this time
The stars were brighter, happier
He knew somehow it would be okay
So he pulled aside the girl on the bridge
Alone in her own thoughts
And showed her the planets
They called to her so I called them out name by
name
Thank you she said
And that's when I knew
she too
needed to know it was going to be okay

Embraced

Hold onto me my love
your time has just begun
I know it's hard but there's no time to run

Raindrops

The splash of the rain
against the window
Paints the picture of you
Of us
Falling and falling
Endless directions
Colliding and passing
Fast or slow
When it comes to a end
When the water runs out
Where does that energy go

Confidence

I could feel the eyes turning as she graciously
made herself present
A gorgeous flower in the snow
Unexpected but miraculous
Her beauty was well known

Confidence Pt. 2

7

I could feel the eyes watching as I
Stumbled into the crowded room
A weed in a field of flowers
just waiting to be torn away
My presence unknown

Fingernails

A broken fingernail
No pain at first glance
Just cut it file it away
And your fingers will have a chance
But if one is shorter
don't they all have to be
Because equity of fingernails
Will keep me at peace
So I bite them shorter
First more violent then the last
It becomes a habit to help me
Erase away the past

So what happens when it stops
Can I let them grow
But they're jagged and gross
And I don't want you to know
If I file them down
to the erase marks
How will we know
That we've gotten this far

So a broken fingernail
No pain a first glance
Is the worst kind of temptation
The pain that lasts

Pity Love

So she turned on one foot and said goodbye
This is the truth you're one big lie
All you do is play games
All the time

The fragrance of you

What reminds me of you,
The smell of stolen glances,
Kind gestures,
Forgetful nights,
How I almost fell in love with you,
But something wasn't quite right
And I think that's what hurt me the most
Somehow you were perfect but
Too perfect for me

So it goes…

0-100 life is perfect then it's not
feel like your going no where suddenly you can't
stop
I just want to feel the balance, like rain on a
cloudy day but suddenly is storming and the rain
won't go away
It's 0-100 life is perfect then it's not
Where driving on a freeway and now I can't stop
Push on the breaks we fall apart is this what
happens next
tell me what's the answers because I'm a
fucking wreck

Year 13

Long nights, uber home
Cutting friends and letting go
Is this what life is meant to be

Paperback love

13

It was the little things I watch them do
Reaffirming notions of how he loves you
Unattainable fairy tails I wish could come true
Where girls like me get the guys like you

Pack back love but it's not fiction
He could say that he loves me
I still wouldn't listen
Because he doesn't look at me the look at each
other
They say chivalry is dead guess you're not the
right lover

Fadeaway

Forgetting streets of a place you once called
home
Holes in memories of what and who you've
known
Trying to recall you back from the past
I thought those memories would always last

Daddy Issues

She's got daddy issues
Cant commit to you
You find her with a bag
sitting in the bathroom
She says you can't be mine
And that was the line
You know she's messed up
But you get along fine

Perfect

We all wanna be perfect
With pretty hair and perfect faces
Smile and laugh or your to basic
We all wanna be perfect
With perfect figures hourglass
You can't have rolls or your to fat
We all wanna be perfect

But what is perfect
It's standard we create to hurt ourselves
It doesn't exists not even in god himself
We spend our lives tryna be like magazines
Edited and retouched to the extremes

Your perfect no matter what you look like
It may be hard but this is your fight
We're amazing and perfect to ourselves
No matter what anyone says themselves

Utopia

How much time
Will it take
For our souls to break
In this world we imagined and

How many more
Life's will fall
Does it matter at all
To this world we imagined

hurricane

The soft breeze of an ocean
holds back my emotions
one breath is my gift for you
take it now put it to use

Self sabotage

Standing there with a loaded gun
finger on the trigger before it's even begun
Crimson lies on the floor
And I just hope to god we weren't meant for
more than this pain in my chest
they call it love but I call it regret

To the love of my life

There was a point in time
We're I wanted to commit
Not necessarily suicide
but something like it
it wasn't quite that I wanted to die
but more so the fact there was no point to
survive

So it makes me wonder why I'm even here
Surrounded by blank people and endless fear
Do I have a purpose or is it just for fun
Stuck people watching until I find the one